Dying to Live
A Journey Beyond the Mind

by
Michael Lindsay

*Rabbi Friedman,
Thanks for your
encouragement!
— Mike*

Published by Inform Creative Services

Copyright © 2004 Michael Lindsay

All rights reserved.
No part of this book may be reproduced or utilized
in any form or by any means, electrical or mechanical,
without permission in writing from the publisher.

INFORM
CREATIVE SERVICES

Published by
Inform Creative Services
1406 Park Drive
Raleigh, NC 27605
www.dyingtolivebook.com

Library of Congress Control Number: 2003097159

ISBN: 0-9746198-3-3

Printed in the United States of America

Without my cocoon,
without my thumb in this life;
this book would not exist.

Wind touches water,
and a ripple is born.

Male and female touch,
and a child is born.

The ripple grows into a wave,
and the child into an adult.

While born from them,
a wave is neither water nor wind.

It is its own form.

Yet it moves through the water
by the power of the wind.

And so we move through life,
by the power of the Creator.

A wave swells and rises as it nears the shore.
We grow and mature as we age.

When we reach the shore of our destiny,
the wave breaks and our life ends.

Washed ashore,
our energy helps shape a world we don't yet know.

In the struggle to survive,
we create the stress that defines us.

As a raindrop on a leaf clings to itself,
we hold on to our self image.

But it is only surface tension,
this edge of our consciousness.

As one drop touches another,
the tension is broken.

One flows into the other,
until they each no longer exist.

We become a cascade of reconnecting,
from one drop to the ocean.

A bird falls to the ground.
To fly again, it must stand.

Standing, it starts to walk.
Walking, it starts to run.

Running, it learns to survive.
Living on the ground, it forgets to fly.

The bird's true nature becomes a distant memory.
The sky becomes a dream.

Form blinds us to Reality.
Sensing its borders,
we believe its truth.

But that's only the half of it.
A half-truth,
which is not enough.

More is desired.
Many attempt satisfaction
with more half-truths.

A futile effort.
An infinite number of half-truths
can never equal the Truth.

The Truth is boundless.
Reality is beyond the boundaries of form.
Discovered by the senses,
form is known by the mind.
Reality is beyond the mental maps of our making.

The discovery of Truth
begins when we put down our maps of half-truths.

Do we seek God,
or does God find us?

Do we push harder,
or do we yield?

Like a bubble rising through water,
we are naturally drawn upward.

As air expands in its ascent,
so we grow through life.

Ever growing, ever expanding; but separate.

When the bubble breaks the surface,
its destruction is its release.

When we reach our life's end,
our death is our release.

No longer separate,
we become one.

Desires fulfilled,
or desires controlled.

Sensory pleasure,
or senses focused.

Mind busy,
or mind aware.

Ego enhanced,
or ego dissolved.

Holding on, life becomes death.
Letting go, death becomes life.

Sheared from the Lamb,
we are born.

As the Creator's wool,
we are woven.

Minds like needles, sharp and focused;
hearts like threads, flexible and yielding;
a perfect cloth can be made.

Minds dull and confused,
hearts hardened and unbending;
the fabric of life is torn.

Our death ties the knot,
Creation does not fray.

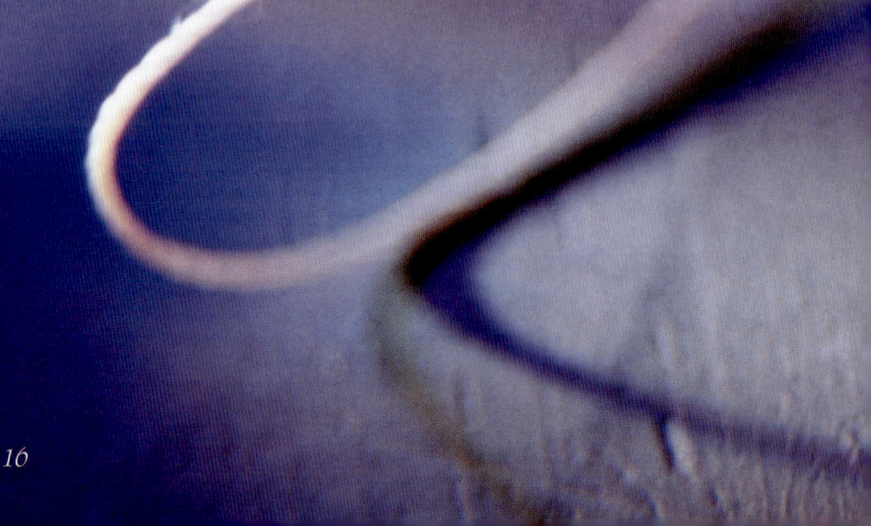

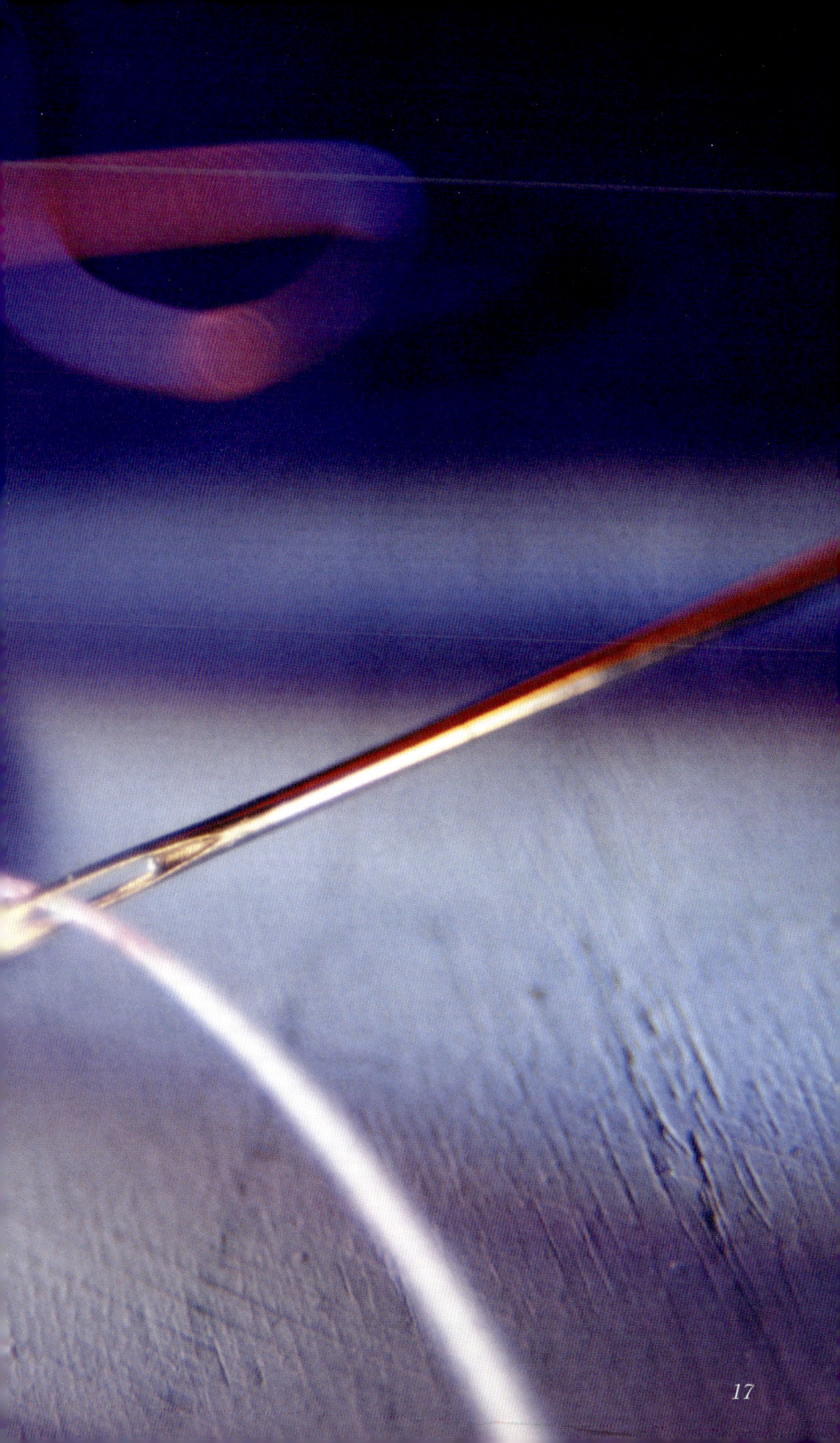

Attempting to do the will of God,
some impose their will on others.

They believe this will make others righteous.
They believe this will make the world right with God.

However:

Righteousness cannot be imposed.
It is born in a world of free will.

Without the ability to choose good from evil,
righteousness doesn't exist.

The confines of my body,
strengthen it for my life's run.

The arrogance of my self,
free me from its bondage.

Rather than race with self determination.
Let me move in unison with what is real,
but seldom seen.

Locked within the atom,
lies the energy of the sun.

To release this energy,
the atom must yield to force.

In the process of yielding,
its form is destroyed.

And its energy is released.

Locked within each of us,
lies the energy of Creation.

To release this energy,
we must yield to its source.

In the process of yielding,
our selves are destroyed.

And our potential is released.

Begging when we should be praying,
we will never know the Unknown.

Ask for nothing, and receive guidance.
Revelation is its own reward.

Prayer is not a dialogue between us and the Creator.
It is an openness to the the Unknown's will.

As the hand does what the mind wants,
we must learn to be.

Pride is misplaced authorship,
or accomplishment that is meaningless.

Reaching beyond our boundaries,
we can touch Creation.

It is from there that genuine accomplishment springs,
and it is to there that we belong.

I ache to know what is Unknown.
My senses only half fill me.

I want to know You completely,
yet I am afraid to lose myself.

My mind confines me to its cage.
I am safe, but alone.

In a leap of faith,
we plunge into this world.

Treading water,
some of us survive.

Swimming,
some of us prosper.

Yet all suffer from the world's storms,
that blow across the water's surface.

Struggling to breathe,
we fight to stay afloat.

Yet beneath this stormy surface,
the water is calm.

Submerging ourselves while breathing,
being calm while the storm rages.

Losing ourselves while living.
There lies the next leap of faith.

In a moment of weakness,
I desire to be strong.

Fearing the unknown,
I want to control the world.

Unable to command what is beyond me,
I lose self-control.

Constricted to my self,
I wither on the vine.

In a moment of awareness,
I lose the desire to control.

Loving the unknown,
I experience a new world.

Seeing what is beyond me,
I lose my self.

Touching the source of life,
I mature on the vine.

I think of You often,
yet I don't know You.

I used to talk to You,
when I thought I knew You.

Then it was You, Me, and Them;
now it is Us.

Gone are the easy definitions
and the meaning they gave.

But also gone
are the divisions they caused.

Crossing over meaningless borders,
All is accessible, All is One.

If your goal is a life without pain,
your aim is too low.

Pain is a teacher.

Through its lessons,
we learn the difference between health and disease.

As a guide,
it leads us on the path to health.

A life spent in the avoidance of pain
is a life without direction.

Use pain like a map:
study it for direction,
it will guide you through life.

37

I deny the background sound,
pounding on my mind.

I drown it out with diversions,
more work, more stuff, more pleasure.

But the knocking won't stop,
and my desire for more is never satisfied.

I already know deep down,
I must answer that knocking.

Why do I ignore it,
why do I seek diversions?

I must unlock the door,
and open up.

What am I afraid of?
The door is not real.

What do I have to lose?
Reality is beyond the confines of my mind.

39

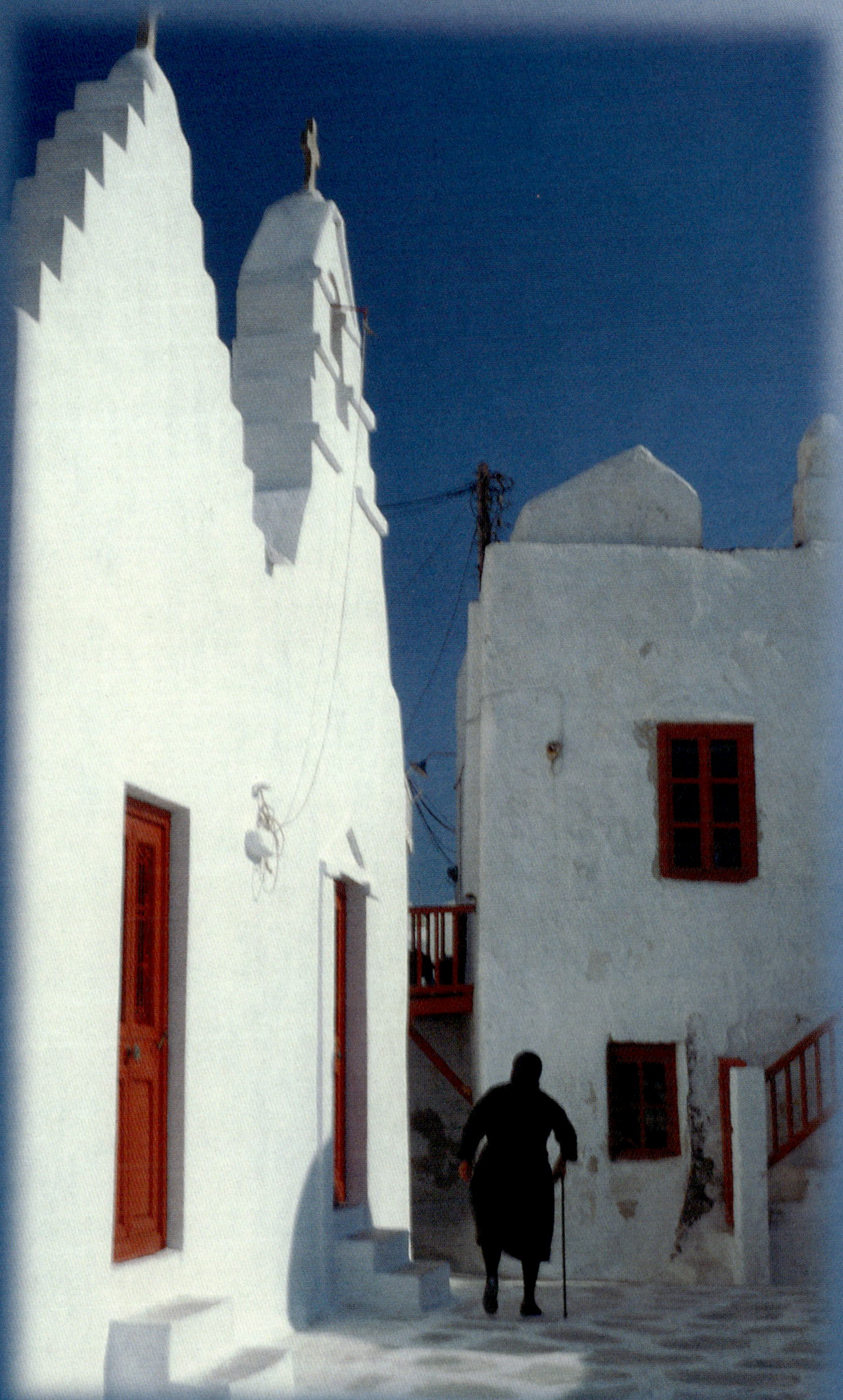

The comfort of home,
where wrongs are made right.

The cocoon of childhood,
where we're told wrong from right.

We grow and mature;
and leave it forever.

We grow old and tired;
and seek it forever.

Mothers and fathers,
please always be there for them.

The way they walk on solid ground,
your children will take your support for granted.

As ever present as the air they breathe,
they will assume your love is always there.

You are the cornerstone of their hearts.
You are the keystone of their minds.

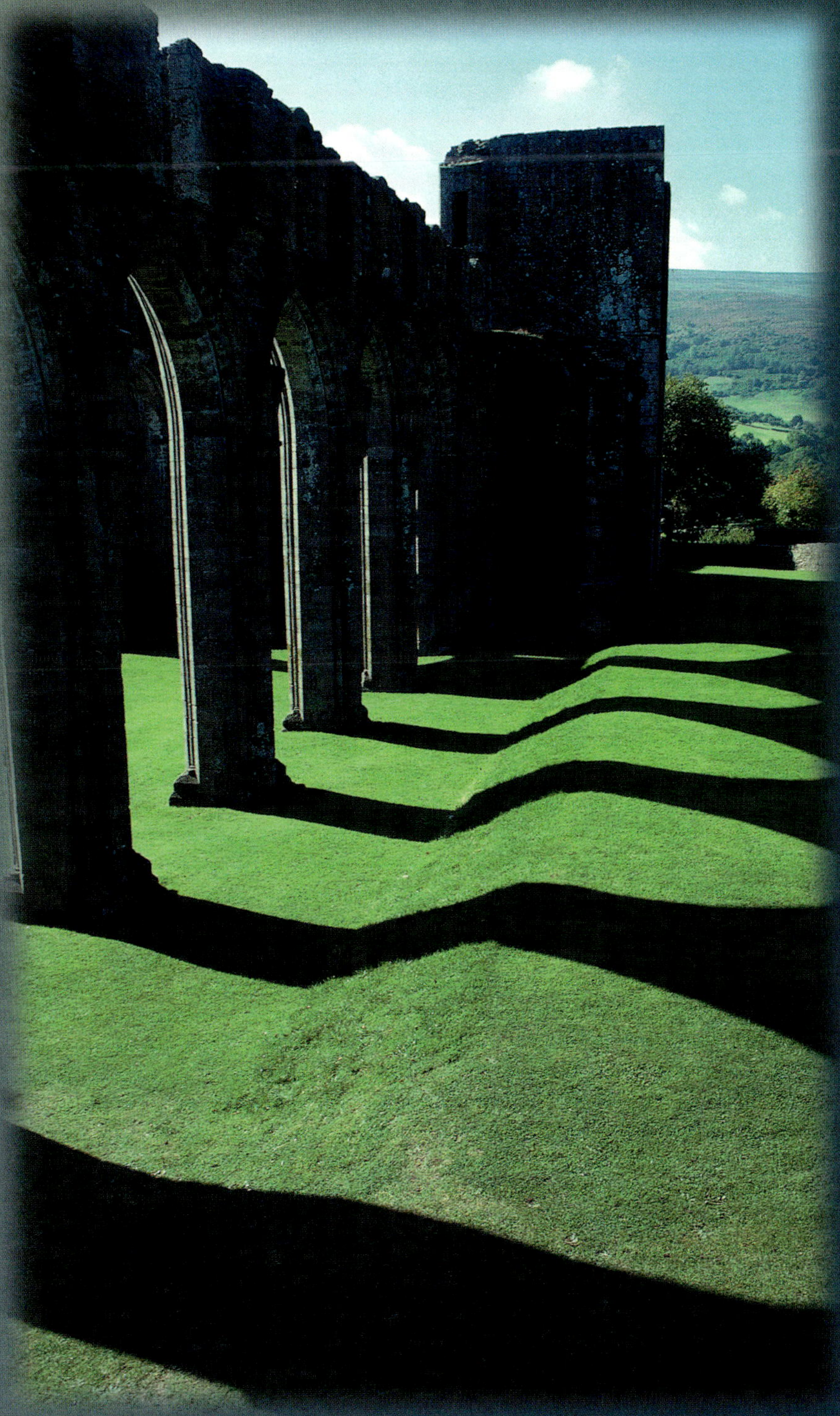

Fire walls of brick and mortar,
we put them up to protect our buildings.

Fire walls of the emotions,
we develop them to protect our hearts.

While they protect,
they also contain.

What we keep in,
we also keep out.

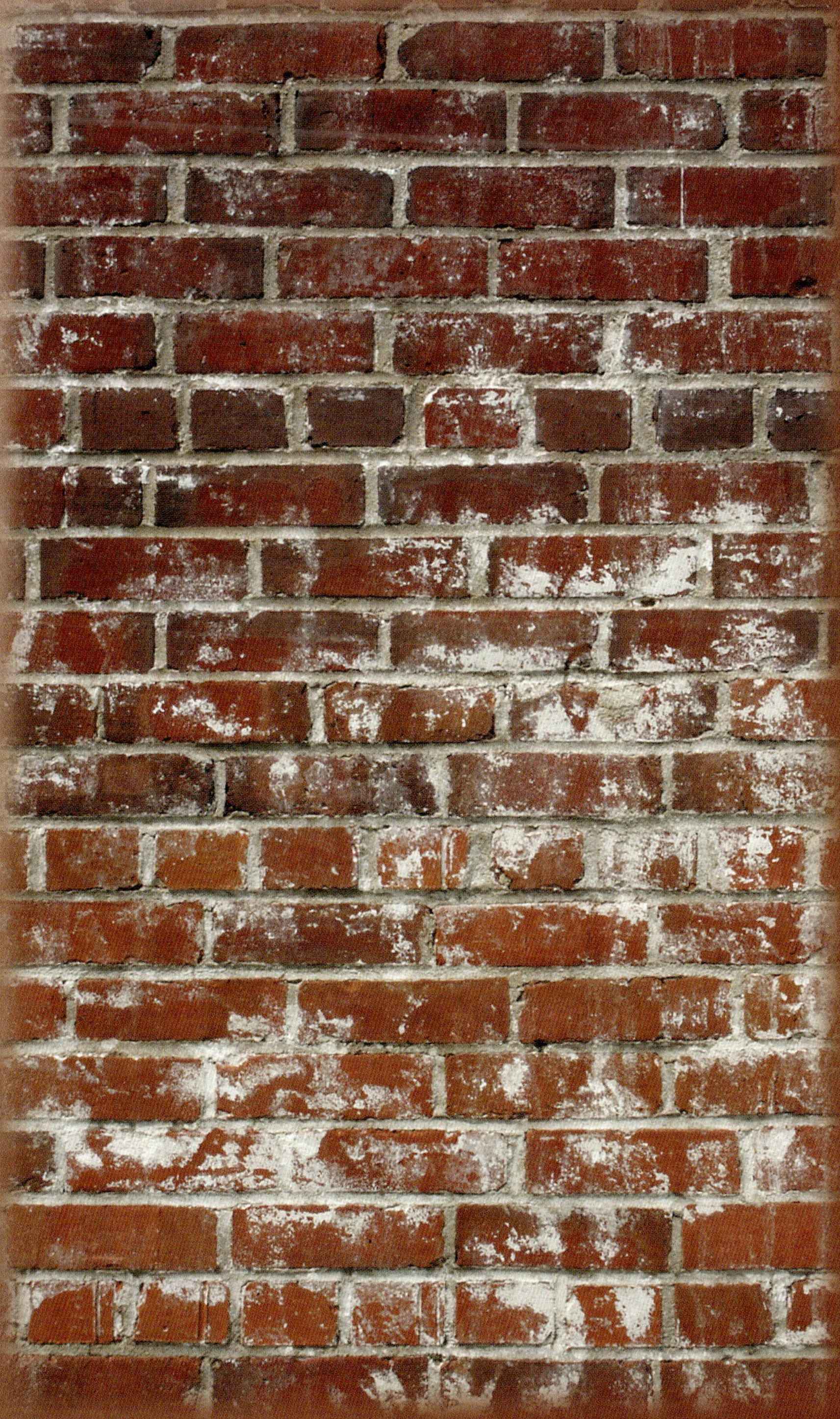

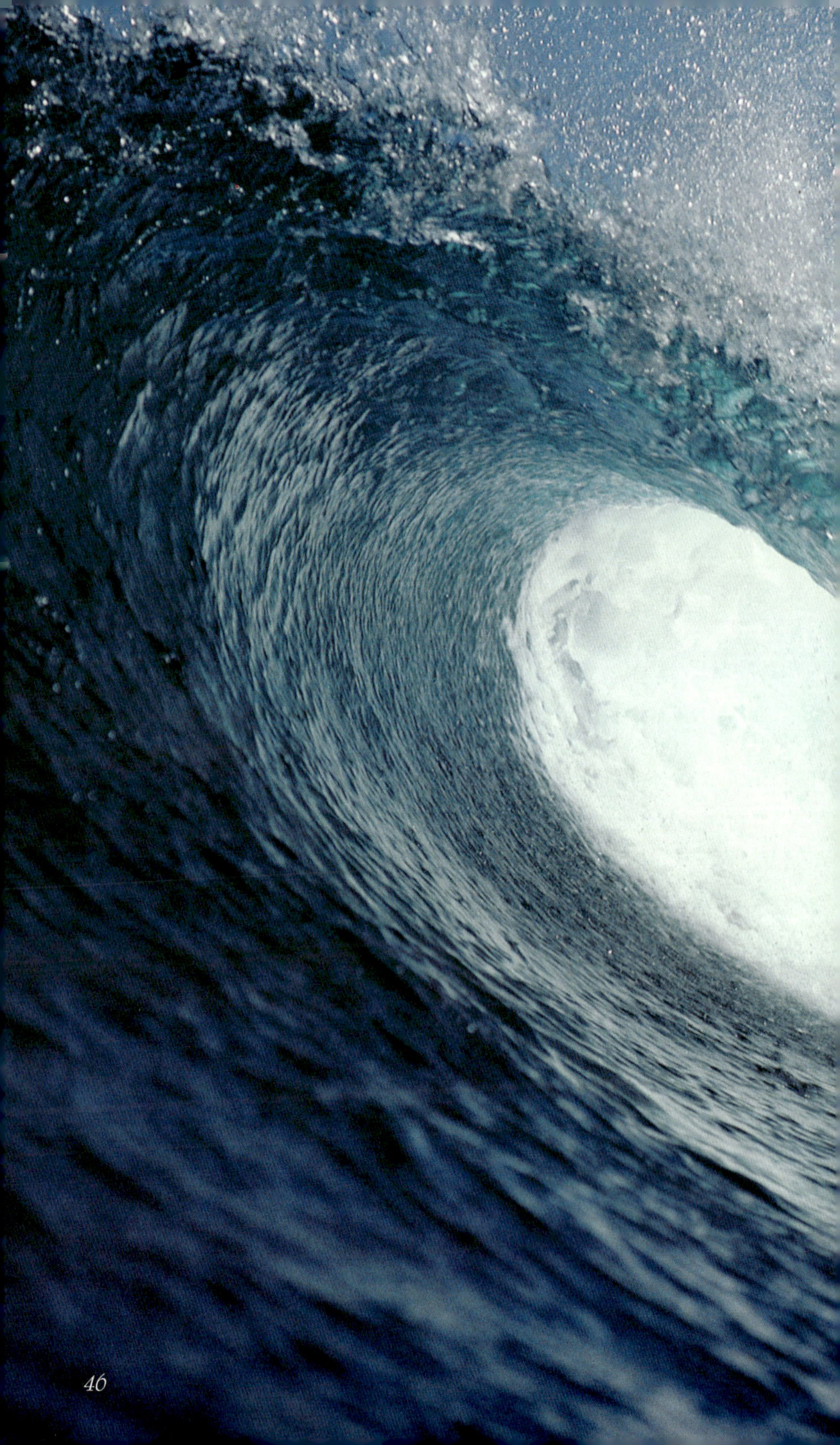

Standing firm in the ocean's surf,
we keep our balance only in the smallest of waves.

The larger waves pick us up,
and push us down.

Thrashing about,
we fight the ocean's power.

Letting go and flowing with the waves,
their energy becomes our energy.

Surrendering ourselves,
we ride the crest of life.

Let us move watchfully through life,
studying the effects of our actions.

While hard to see,
our efforts impact beyond our knowledge.

So be cautious when the world calls,
and moves us to act hastily.

Be alert to the desire to be strong,
and push for quick results.

A stone may be strong and water may yield,
as the pounding surf breaks upon the rocks.

But remember this:

Although a glacier moves slowly,
its frozen water can cut rock.

50

Awake to our work,
we forget our dreams.

Working for a living,
we lose our life.

Busy with the chores of the day,
we miss the path to tomorrow.

I rejoice in my struggle,
it sharpens my mind.

I give thanks for my pain,
it opens my heart.

I am moved by life,
it transforms my self.

I am lifted by death,
it releases my soul.

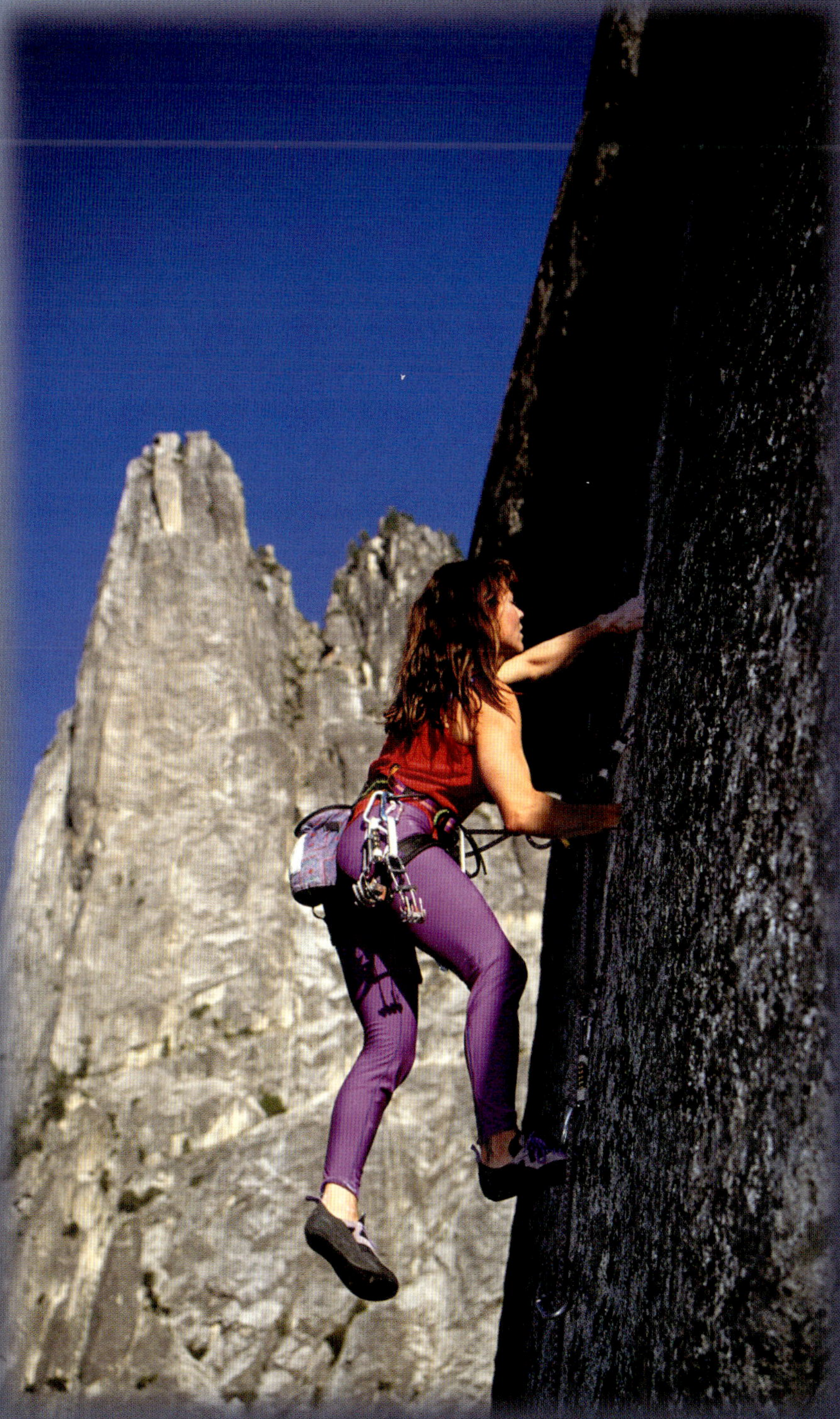

Energy and form.
Heaven and earth.

Energy becomes form.
Form becomes energy.

All are one.

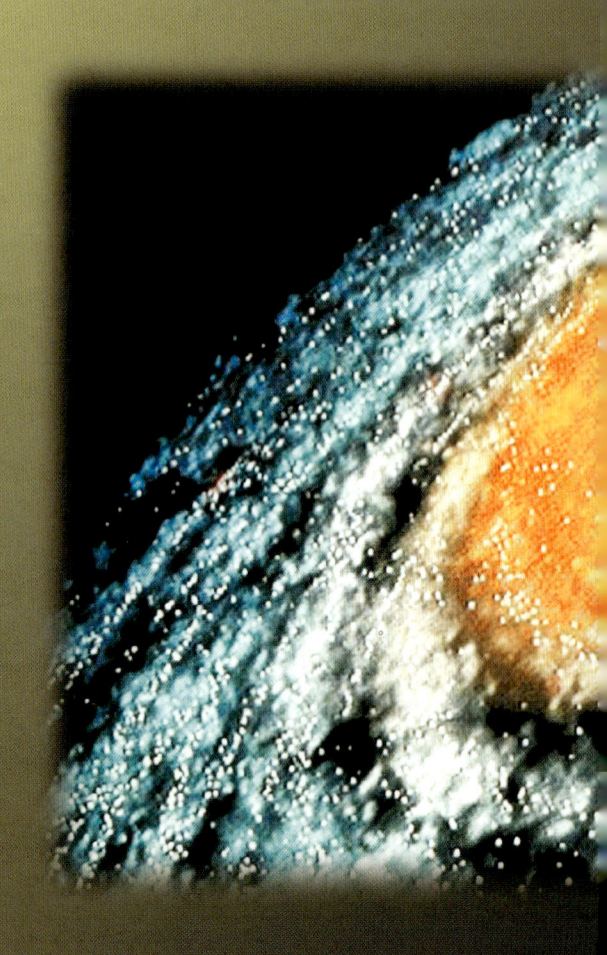

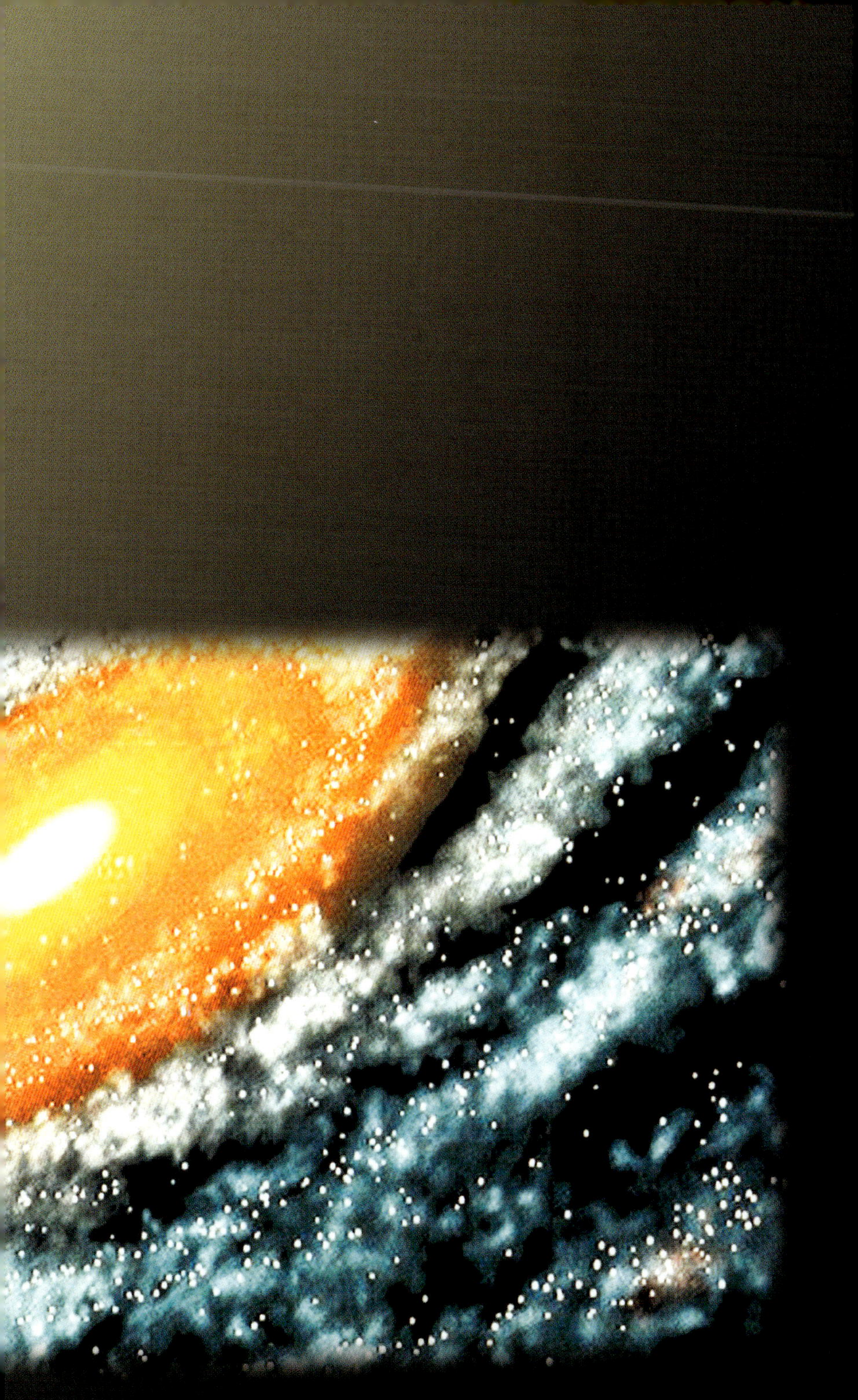

I clean myself,
only to wallow in self pity.

I purge myself,
only to flounder with desire.

A cycle of awareness and despair.
Can this chain be broken?

I see the way in fleeting moments.

Then I return to self destructive ways,
and despair consumes me once more.

When will I stop struggling,
and accept what is to be?

When will I reject this illusion,
and accept the Reality that's beyond my ability?

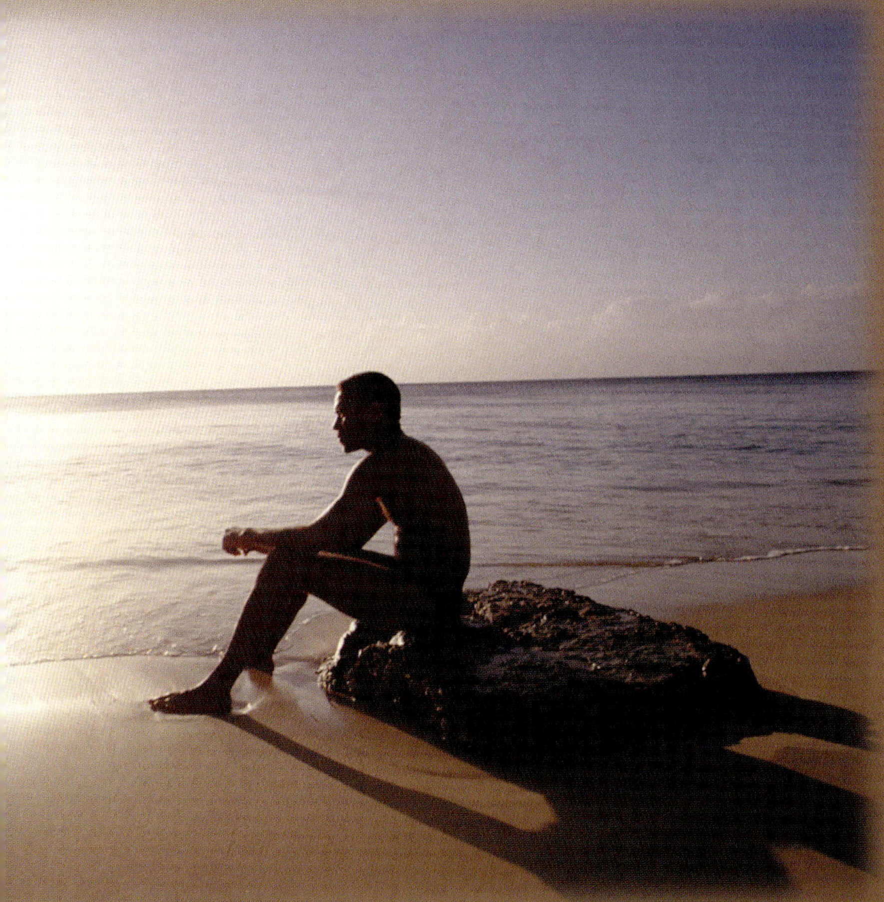

My heart has never been completely in this world.
Yet to survive I must understand its rules.

Half-heartedly, I learn these lessons.
But it is only knowledge for subsistence.

When will I commit to the real lesson plan?
And reap the rewards of insight.

When will I accept my assignment?
And be free of my fear.

59

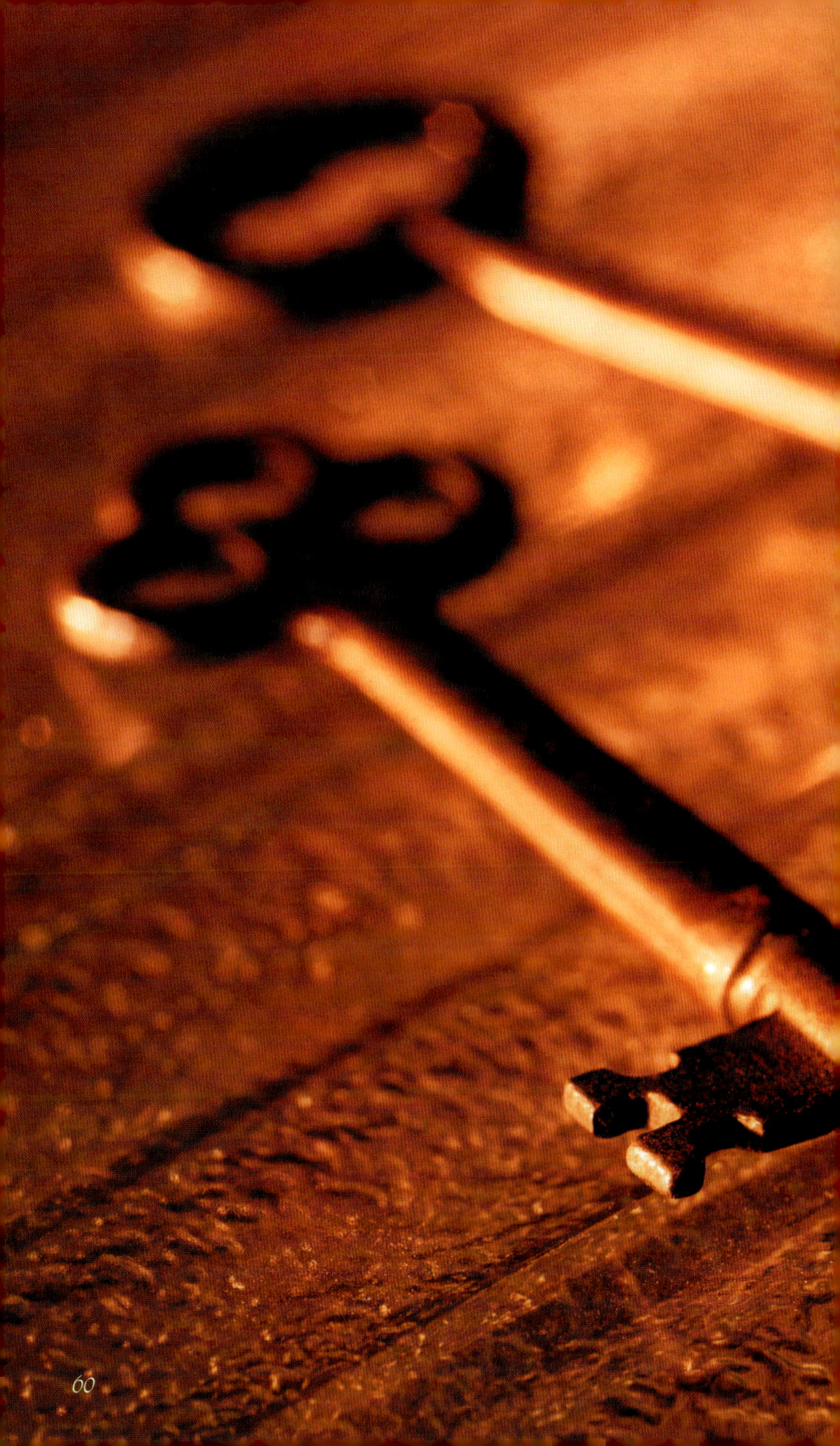

Aimless in a life of pleasure,
I never move beyond myself.

Trying to avoid pain,
my spirit becomes lazy.

I become a prisoner,
never knowing the real world.

Pain is the key,
it unlocks the door to Reality.

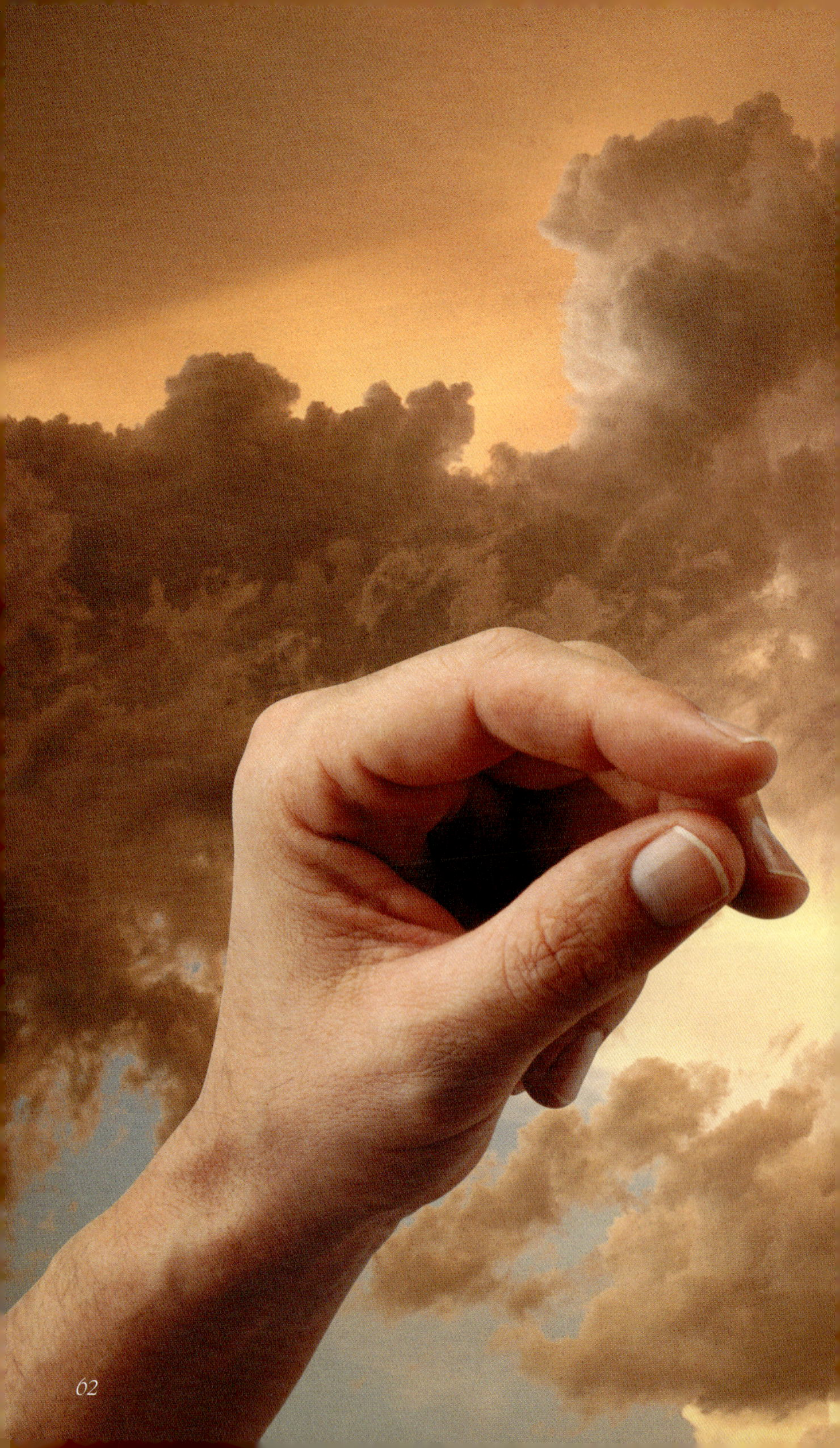

Before you and I became one,
I was like a finger without a thumb.

Grasping at living,
but not taking hold.

United, we have a hand in creation.
Together, we create a new world.

I keep trying to be this or that.
Pursuing one goal then another.

Trying to please others or trying to please myself.
Struggling until my energy gives out.

When will I learn to just be.
To allow myself to become what is destined.

Moved by the power of Creation.
My real self, my real purpose is revealed.

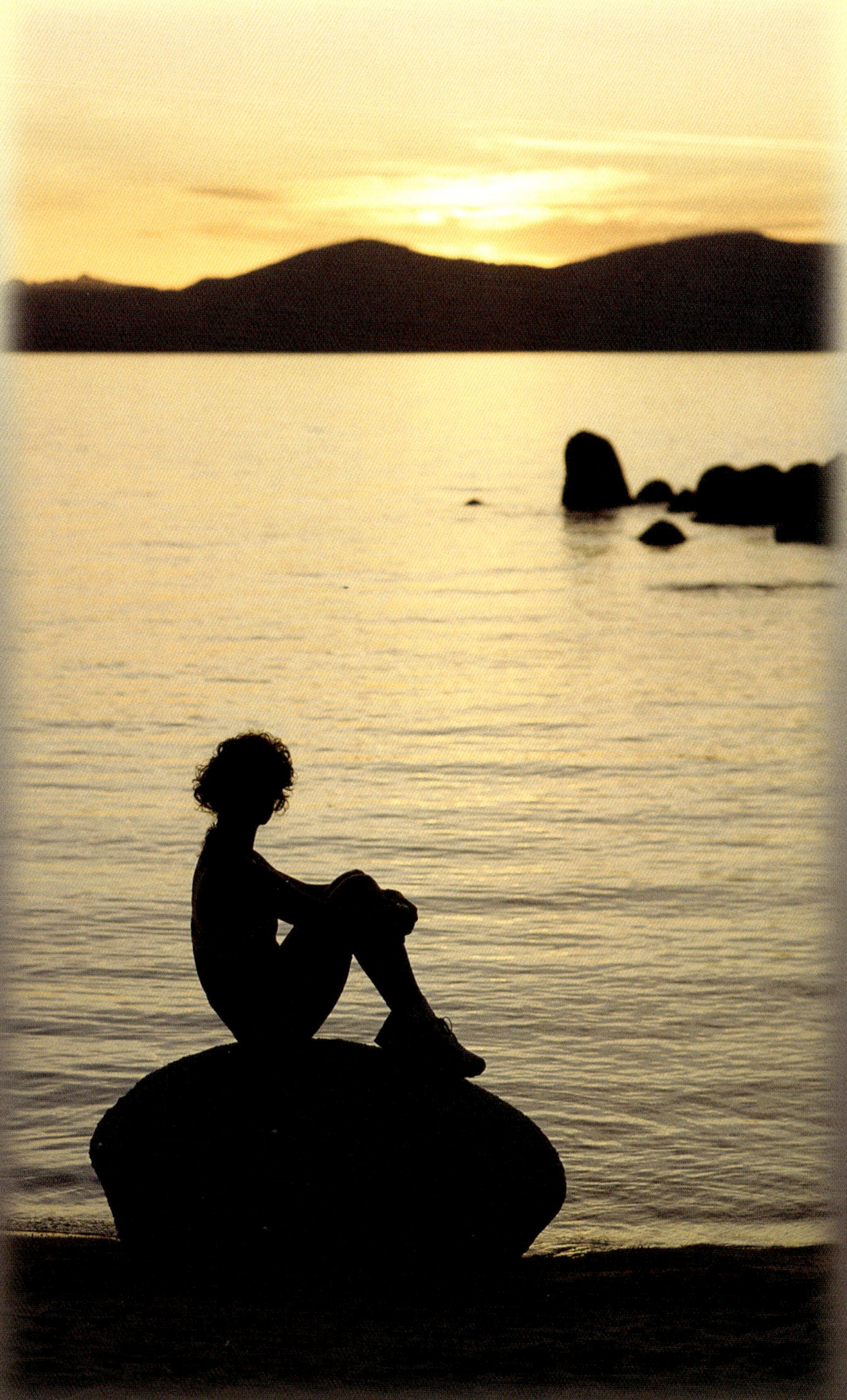

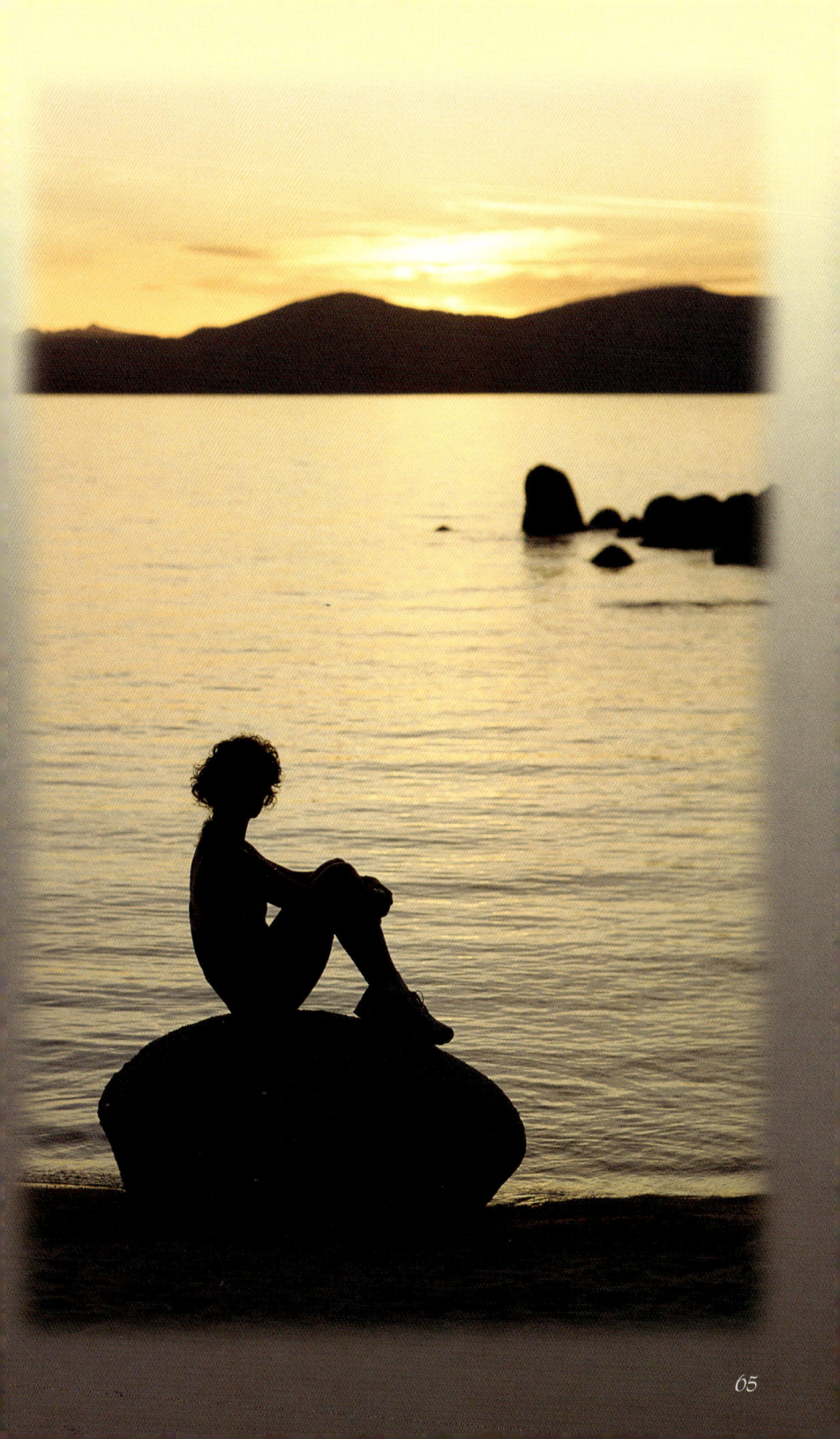

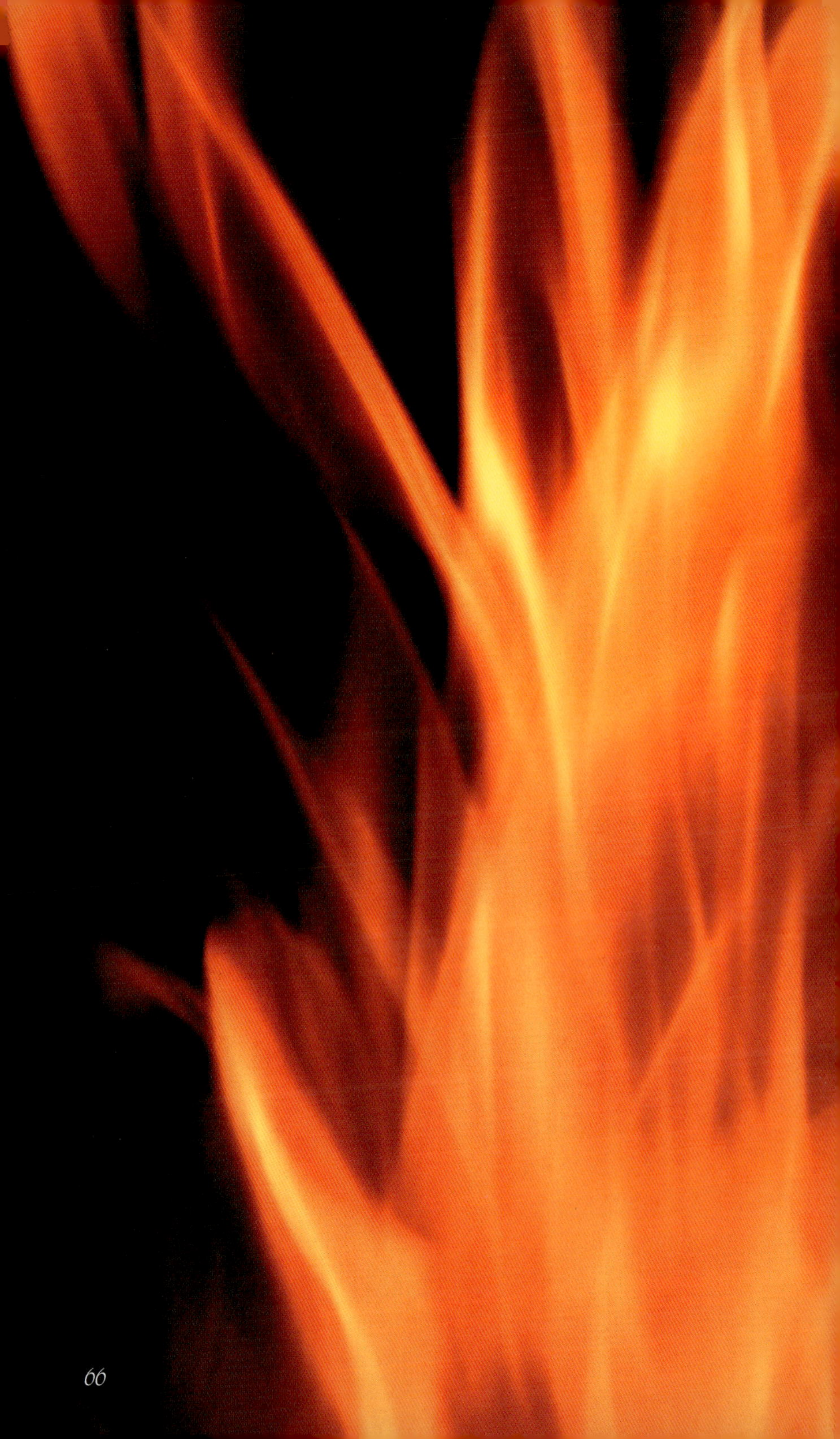

If pleasure makes me happy,
why is more of it never enough?

And if I couldn't feel pain,
wouldn't I walk too close to the flame?

What if I had to choose between:
a life of pleasure or a life of pain.

Would I choose a life of comfort,
hiding and imprisoning myself forever.

Or would I choose a life of suffering,
destroying myself in the fire.

Please give me a life long enough and tough enough,
to discover who You are, who We are, and who I am.

Only then will I know,
I can touch the flame without getting burned.

A world of shadows,
we see only the effect but not the cause.

The more we see ourselves in each other,
the closer we get to the source of love.

As the boundaries of our selves become blurred,
the more in focus becomes the Unknown.

69

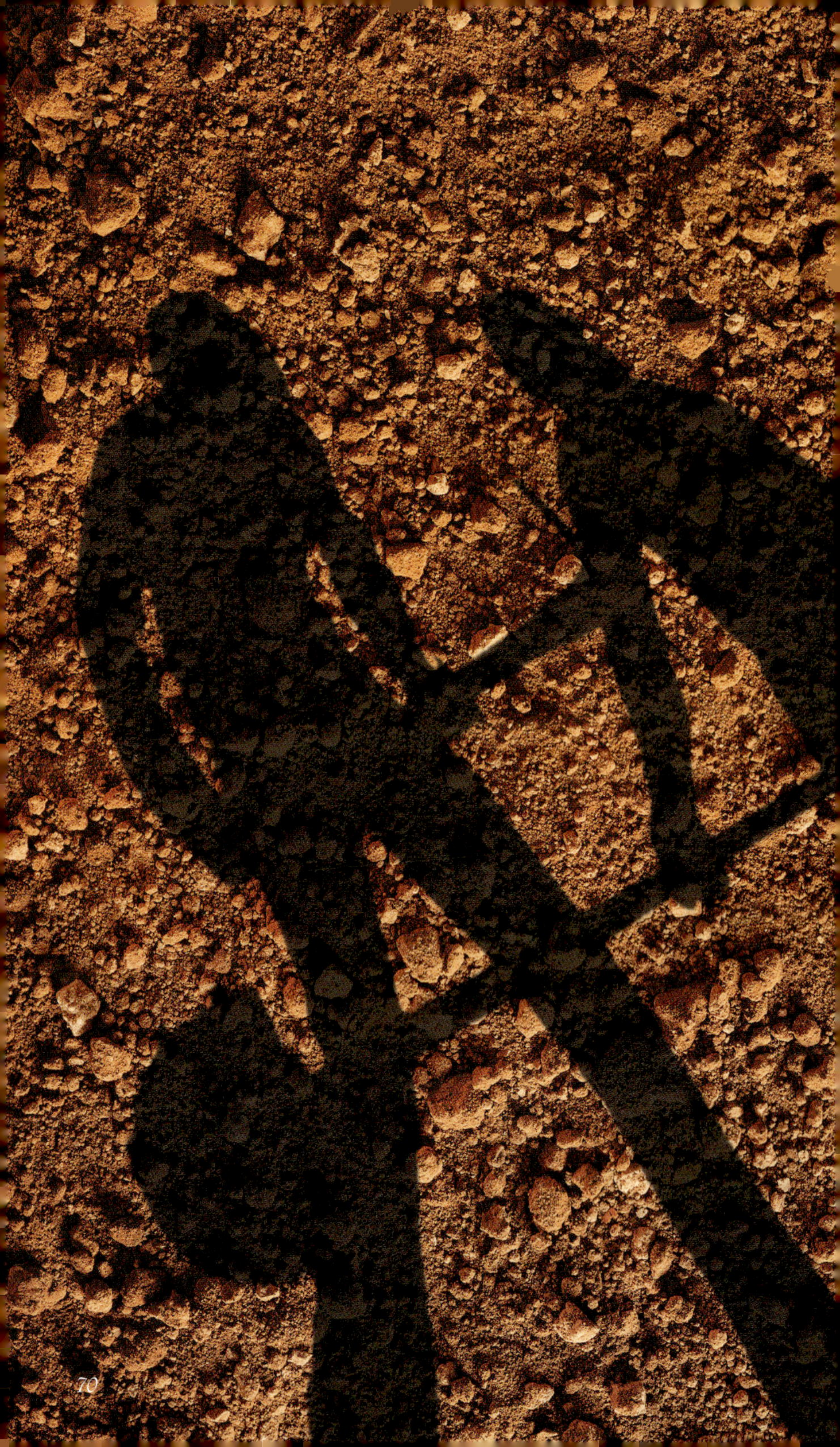

We should give thanks for our pain and suffering.
They are our tools for revelation.

Like a pick ax and shovel,
the more we use them, the deeper we dig.

Layer after layer,
deeper and deeper

From the known to the Unknown,
revealing the true nature of Reality and ourselves.

Desires and worries cloud my mind,
a fog envelopes my soul.

I must climb out of myself,
and rise above the clouds.

Standing in Creation's light,
the fog is lifted.

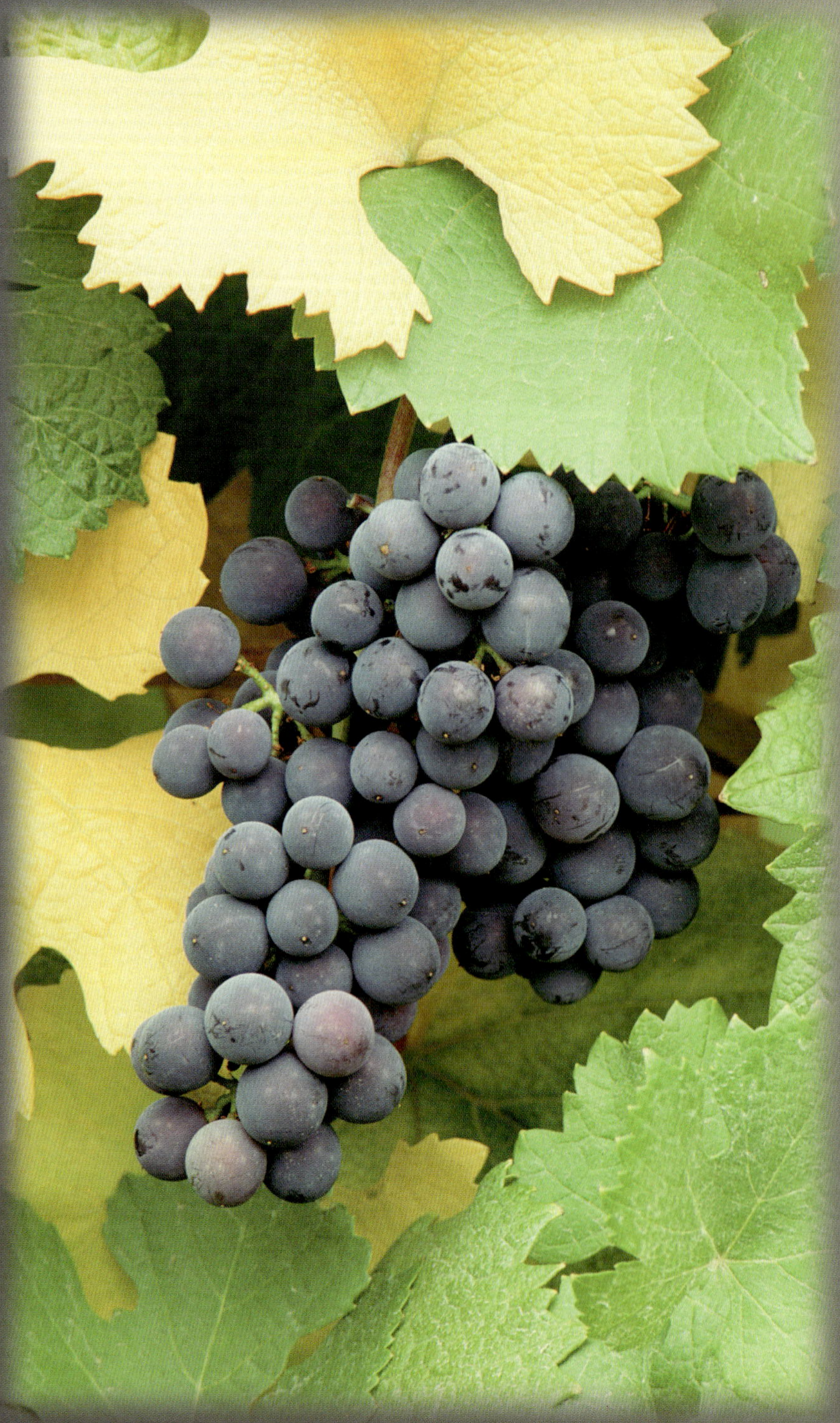

Some of us are dying to live,
others are living only to die.

Withering on the vine,
we offer nothing in return.

Maturing on the vine,
we become the seed of Creation.

Born as unbelievers,
we grow to believe the world's truth.

Trusting our senses,
we move through life.

Facing a senseless death,
can we learn to see?

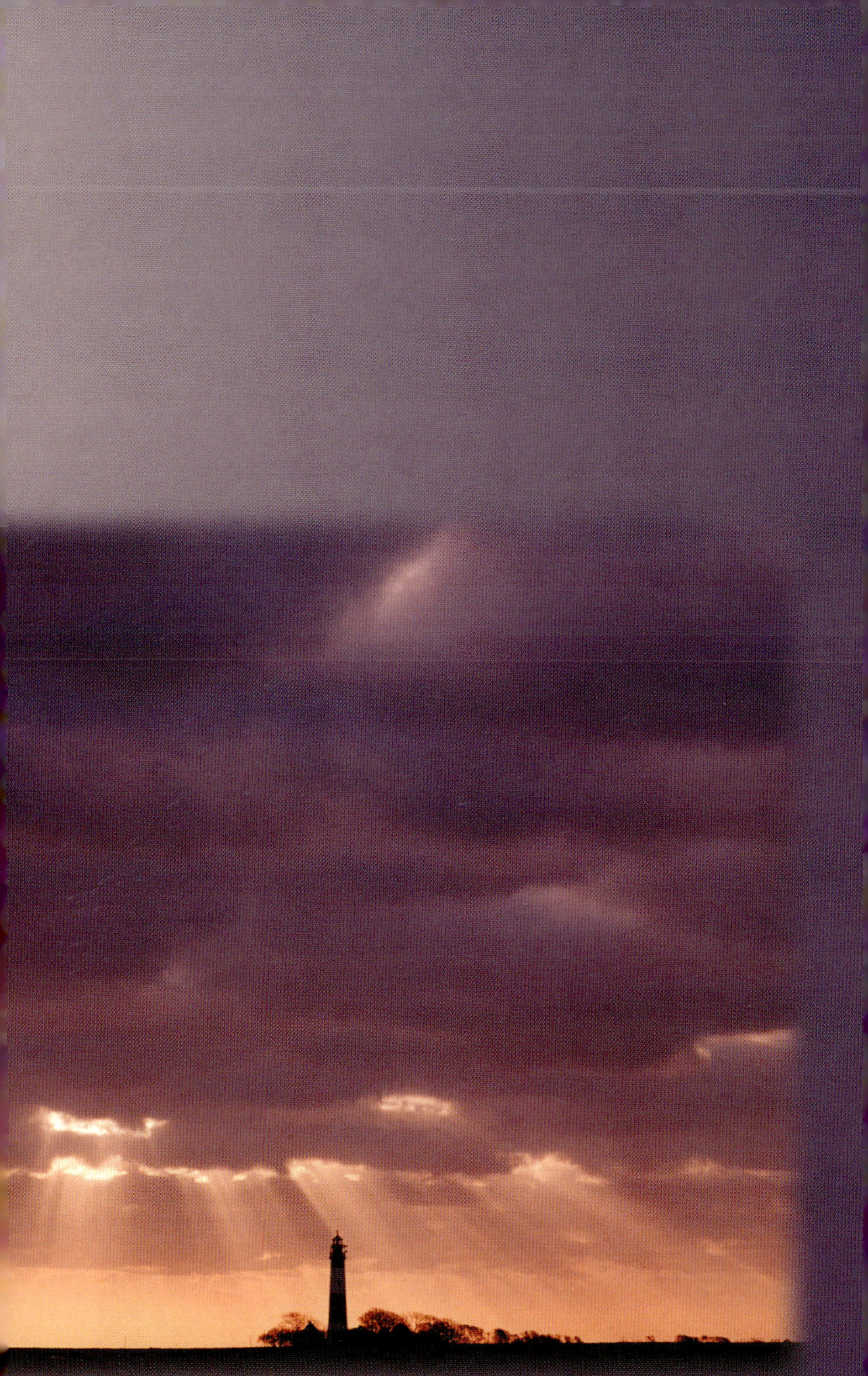

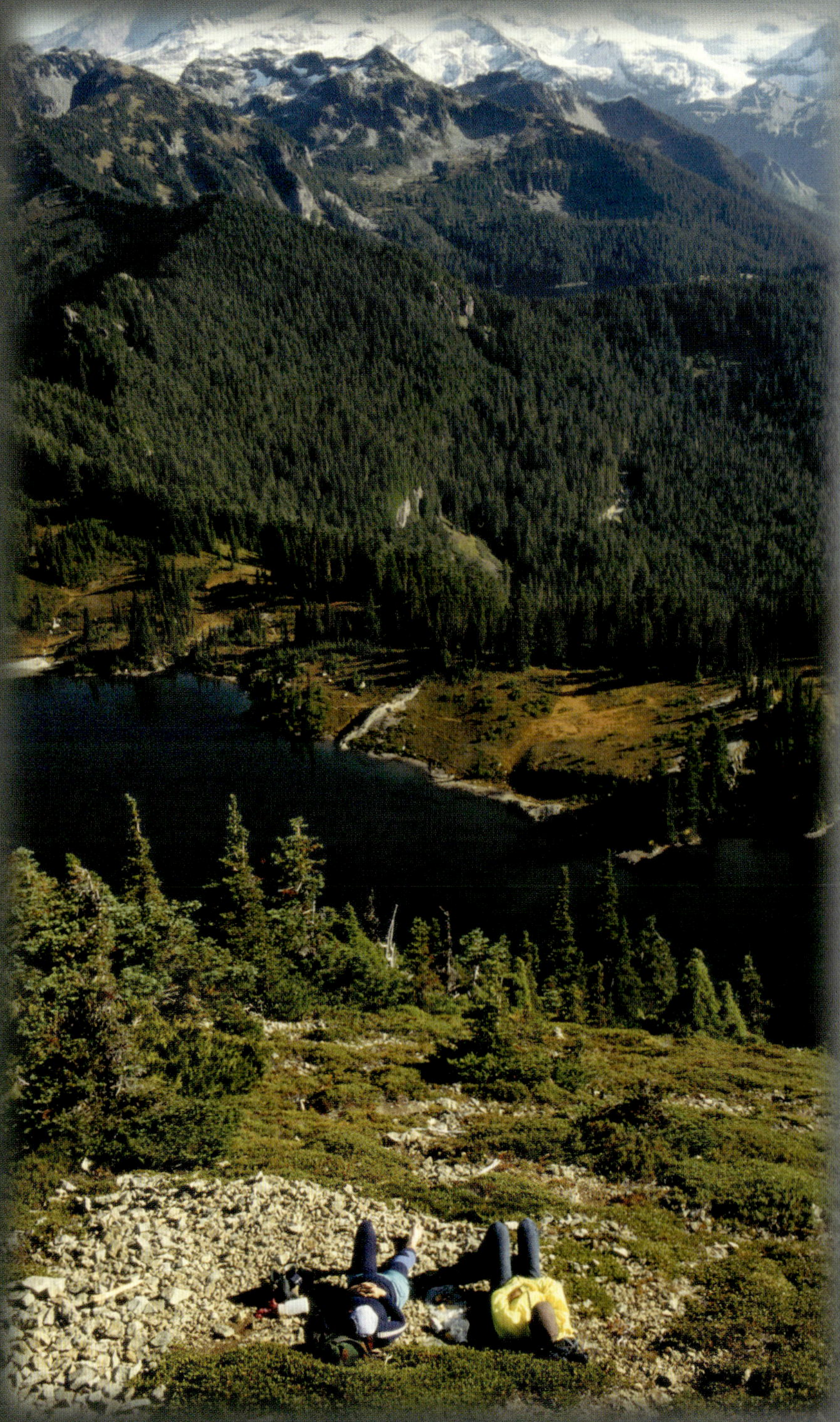

We can't be made to love,
we each travel our own path.

When pulled by love,
our view becomes clear.

When pushed by desires,
Our vision becomes cluttered.

Confused by the objects of our desires,
we lose our way.

We make mountains out of molehills,
and miss the real mountain views.

Love is the path of least resistance.
Free of clutter, our path is clear.

You have helped me to become
more than I am alone.

You have helped me to become
something I can give back.

You are my first surrender.
Creation will be the second.

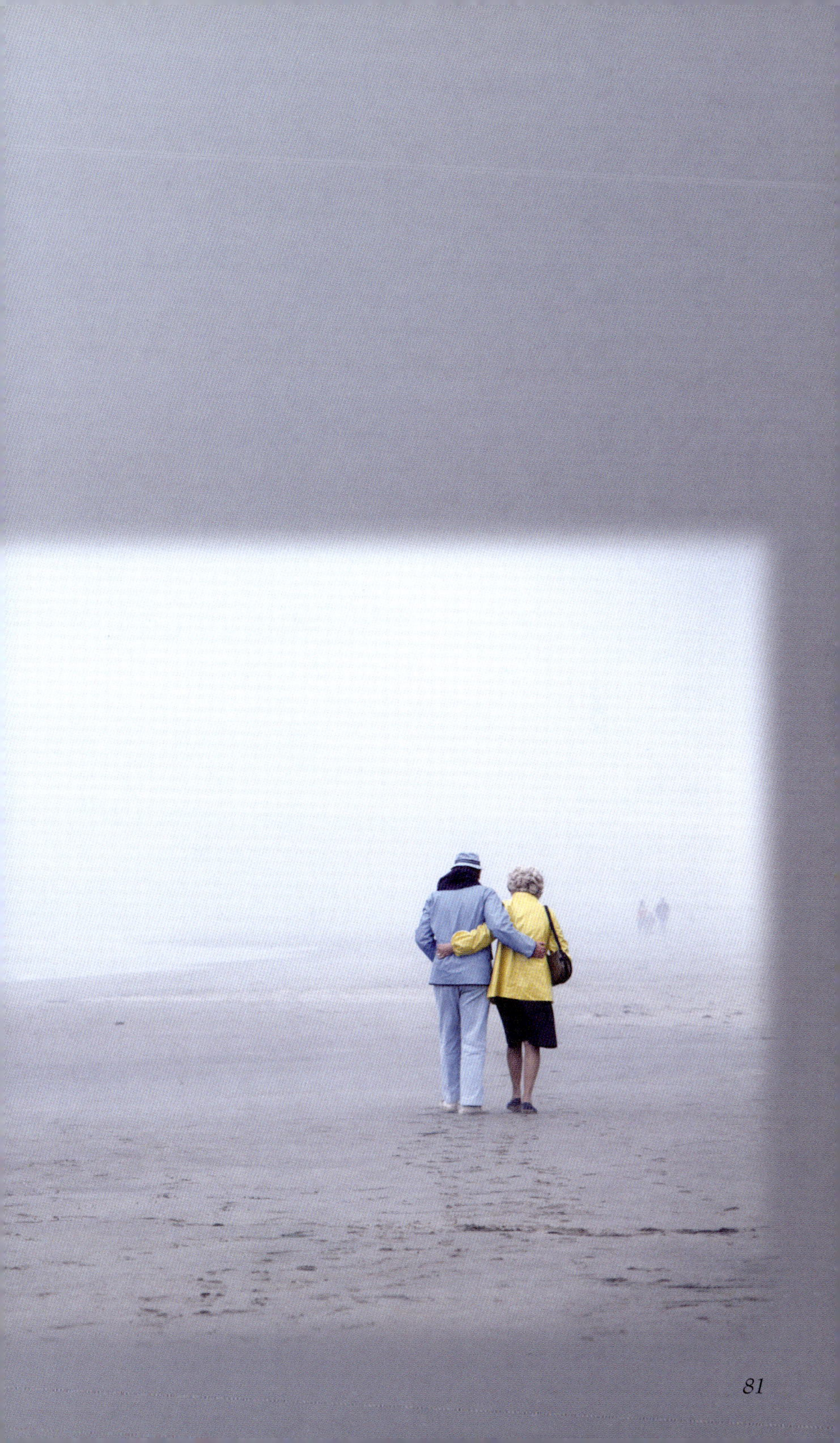

82

A gardener listens to a voice deep within,
where it resonates with a sound we can't hear.

It is the sound of Creation,
it is the future garden path we do not know.

When the gardener and his creation become one,
the plans of the Creator become clear.

The landscape achieves a balance,
that could not occur without an active hand.

But the hand is not the gardener's,
it is the hand of the Creator.

The gardener is the hand in motion.

I sense a distant vibration
moving through this place and time.

I desire to know it and hold on to it,
but must let it go.

In harmony with that distant vibration,
I must learn to flow.

Like the rain,
we are born.

Streams turn into rivers,
and so we grow.

The rivers flow into the sea,
and we into death.

The waters are united,
our illusion of separation is dissolved.

As a fellow traveler of this world, I hope you find this book of use. These 44 poems were selected from the notes of my own journey. Most of them were written from 1992 to 2002. In 45 years, I've traveled over a good part of the world. First with my family and now with my wife, Nancy. Along the way, I have met people of many faiths or no faith; all expressing the same hopes and fears. As I read the world's religious books and scientific writings, I see the same desire for the Truth. I hope your journey leads to its discovery.

— Michael Lindsay 9/27/03